This book is dedicated to all who find Nature not an adversary to conquer and destroy, but a storehouse of infinite knowledge and experience linking man to all things past and present. They know conserving the natural environment is essential to our future well-being.

MAMMOTH CAVE
THE STORY BEHIND THE SCENERY®

by Joy Medley Lyons

Joy Medley Lyons, a park ranger at Mammoth Cave National Park, earned her B.A. in English and Creative Writing from Western Kentucky University. Further studies in American History and Folk Studies have meshed with Joy's lifelong love of writing, giving her the opportunity to assist in preserving our nation's cultural and natural heritage.

Mammoth Cave National Park, located in south central Kentucky, was first set aside in 1926. In 1972 it was pronounced the longest recorded cave system in the world.

Front cover: Frozen Niagra, photo by Chip Clark. Inside front cover: Waterfall in Raymer Hollow, photo by Kurt Erlanson. Page 1: Ground Hog, photo by M.L. Mc Coy. Pages 2/3: "Gothic Avenue," photo by Robert J. Cetera.

Edited by Mary L. Van Camp. Book design by K. C. DenDooven.

Fifth Printing, 2003

MAMMOTH CAVE: THE STORY BEHIND THE SCENERY © 1991 KC PUBLICATIONS, INC.
"The Story Behind the Scenery"; the Eagle / Flag icon on Front Cover are registered in the U.S. Patent and Trademark Office.
LC 91-60037. ISBN 0-88714-050-5.

*F*rom the time-worn dirt left by ancient rivers to the slender stone pillars of a gothic chapel, the cave seems to whisper the best-kept secrets of the ages.

The Mammoth Cave Story

ROBERT J. CETERA

Caves are quite common all over the world. They are caused by various forces, usually by water, literally dissolving rock over eons of time.

Mammoth Cave National Park is the granddaddy of all cave systems. The total length is still unknown because additional levels, extension and new connects are still being discovered. With over 350 miles of surveyed cave, Mammoth Cave is at least three times longer than any other system in the world.

Visitors can see different formations, such as the Cathedral Dome, on one of many tours available. The system is so extensive that there are several entrances, each sharing a different aspect of the cave. Several tours are available for spelunkers, and another designed for young children aged 8 – 12 years.

Yes, there is life below ground, a lot of it! Over 130 forms of life exist within the cave. Some have adapted to a light-less existence over millenniums of time

Above ground there is also much to see and enjoy. Along the 60 miles of hiking trails within Mammoth Cave National Park you may see wildlife both within the hardwood forest or the open areas. The Green River runs the length of the park, but the river actually runs below the caves, not above them!

At Mammoth Cave National Park you will find a land of intrigue both above and below ground level. The life and beauty of the formations will show you that our world does not stop at our feet.

The highlight of the Wild Cave Tour is when you visit Hovey Cathedral Dome; today commonly known as Cathedral Dome. It was discovered in 1907 by Benjamin Einbigler, William Bransford and Ed Hawkins. When they discovered the cave it is said that the three explorers found footprints on the ground and a signature on a wall with the name and date of Creighton, 1848—though today there is no sign of either.

TOM TILL

Dawn and autumn's earth hues help Green River shed a misty mood.

CHIP CLARK

"Take time to explore – the world above and the world below!"

***E**xhale...hard! Some visitors choose to experience the cave as a contemporary "spelunker" (caver) might. Look tight? It is! Park rangers and other cavers affectionately call this the "Mole Hole."*

CHIP CLARK

The Cave

It's early morning. Last night's cloudburst has ended and you stand dwarfed by lofty tulip poplar boughs, sending your breath into the cool air. You step carefully between the old cemetery monuments and try, sometimes in vain, to read the names etched upon them. The monuments, too, are dwarfed where they stand—limestone sentinels above cave guides and their companions.

You hike down the trail, passing sycamores and oaks, jonquils and phlox. Two chipmunks dance in the leaves near a fallen log, skittering away as you softly approach. A silent doe and her fawn stare quietly from the stream bed. A pileated woodpecker voices indignation, then swoops and glides in its wood-hen way to the hollow pillar that is a dead beech tree.

Privately owned until the 1960s, Great Onyx Cave was carefully maintained by the Cox family.

" The cave has **befriended**...
slave and freed man,
...**soldiers**
and **young** lovers. "

The trail descends and so do you, crossing the swollen waters of a stream. Last night's rain rolls and trickles, first foaming then pouring over the rocks. The water never stops, sloshing between earthen banks as it might splash within a settler's mining pan. Then, abruptly, the stream shoots down into the ground, as if a plug where pulled and a drain opened.

Veering slightly, a little off balance, you meet the cave's time-worn entrance. Pausing, you marvel as others have marveled. The cave has befriended both slave and freed man, both soldiers and young lovers. The spring that runs here has marked the stone roof for centuries, undeterred in its journey to quench the earth's unquenchable thirst.

THOMAS A. SCHNEIDER

Nineteenth-century cave visitors might have donned mustard-colored flannel caving costumes to follow a slave guide into the gaping entrance of Mammoth Cave. Today, park rangers lead curious visitors into the cave's historic entrance, still the only entrance used on tours.

Now, it's down and into the cave. Blue sky meets gray limestone and the miserly but brilliant forest greens reluctantly splash on perching ferns. The cave, in its chilling, stone-still silence, beckons. You respond, as so many have before, by stepping downward—another step follows, and yet another.

Standing alone in the cave's twilight, you rest. Caught beneath the lofty forest and the cave's rambling passages, you look. You listen. The cave's breath cools the damp flesh of your hands, your neck, and your face. You feel a strong kinship with people long dead. Staring into the darkness of the cave, you feel bound to those early woodsmen, bound to slave guides and their owners.

Beneath the cathedral ceiling you are dwarfed by time and by earth. Then, the moment fades and you recognize the powerful music playing above you. Over the cave's arched entrance pours the water, a gentle forest stream strengthened by evening rains. There, in the cool gray solitude of the limestone walls, you hear it—the mighty ancient waters of a river carving rock, creating the cave called "Mammoth."

Ask any geologist or hydrologist what caused their keen interest in earth science and most will give the same response. Their attraction to rocks and water stems from an earlier passion. That passion is caving. Call them "speleologists," "spelunkers" (from the Latin *speleum*, meaning *cave*), or just plain "cavers." Whatever the label, these modern frontiersmen feel the need to slide into tight belly crawls, straddle canyons 30-feet high, and push into darkness like there is no tomorrow.

Mammoth Cave is, to cavers, the granddaddy of them all. Actively explored today, Mammoth Cave has, in past centuries, been an enticing mystery to hundreds of more primitive curiosity seekers. Rich and poor, black men and white, have felt the silent lure of the cave and been drawn into its darkness.

Early guides at Mammoth Cave made a production of showing the cave. Elaborate methods of lighting were developed. Old stories were told, retold and embellished upon. Every rock, nook and vaulted ceiling was given a memorable, if not grandiose, title. But, for all the showmanship and well-honed storytelling, one fact remains the same. No visitor, past or present, can enter the sprawling passages of Mammoth Cave and not be awed by its size. The cave looms high and sweeps wide around, as if to say, "Yes, I *am* here—and here I will stay."

So many questions rush through one's mind! How did it get here? What made it? How long will it stay here? How can something this *big* not collapse?

Those same questions have been asked, and answered, by numerous cave explorers, geologists and other earth scientists during the last two centuries. What seemed obvious and simple fifty years ago has proven more complex to modern students of geology and hydrology.

For years, with a wink and a smile, cave guides and park ranges have thrown out the summation, "a lot of time, and a whole lot of water." But, behind the lightheartedness they know that many more than those two key elements have combined to create what has come to be called the longest cave in the world.

Mammoth Cave's creation has depended upon a combination of several factors. First, the bedrock is exposed at the surface over a large area and has an almost unnoticeable dip. The limestone bedrock in the ridges is protected by insoluble rocks, but regional drainage occurs underground. The layers of bedrock and the erosion of ridges have not caused significant interruption to cave development. The limestone bedding is quite prominent, with few major joints cutting across the beds.

Tubular passages like this one in "Turner Avenue" were formed while completely filled by flowing water. Tube passages seem to "go on forever." Passageways currently feeding water to springs along the Green River are forming the cave's newest tubular areas.

SAM FRUSHOUR

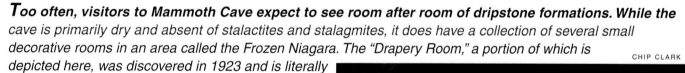

Too often, visitors to Mammoth Cave expect to see room after room of dripstone formations. While the cave is primarily dry and absent of stalactites and stalagmites, it does have a collection of several small decorative rooms in an area called the Frozen Niagara. The "Drapery Room," a portion of which is depicted here, was discovered in 1923 and is literally encased in a variety of limestone travertine formations.

CHIP CLARK

TOM TILL

The magenta hues of a Kentucky sunset blush the peaceful waters of Sloan's Crossing Pond. As night falls, the pond springs to life with the sounds of bullfrogs, cicadas, and other insects. Past generations of cattails and water lilies add to the muck on the pond bottom, gradually replacing the pond water with organic material. Within the next century, the pond will finish its cycle and become a meadow.

"It began with an ancient sea."

During the Paleozoic era, between 600 and 300 million years ago, Kentucky's climate was quite different from the bluegrass region we know today. The continent occupied a spot further south on the globe and resembled a tropical region, much like the Bahamas or the Florida Keys.

During the Mississippian period, 350 million years ago, a sea covered the southeastern portion of the continent. The first vertebrate animals were finding land, and the warm water was depositing still more rock. The sea was teeming with a dense population of tiny organisms whose shells consisted of calcium carbonate. When the organisms died, the hard shells accumulated as sediment, eventually solidifying into fossil-rich limestone.

Over the next 70 million years, roughly 500 feet of limestone was deposited. The Appalachian Mountains continued to push upward in their quest for drier heights. A large river system to the north sprang to life, pushing sand and mud downward into the sea. Some deltas formed, and several hundred feet of sandstone and shale were deposited beneath the warm water.

Roughly 280 million years ago, the sea slowly receded as the continent rose, exposing layers of limestone and sandstone. The earth seemed to roar awake, buckling, stretching and heaving as it shook the water from its still damp surface.

Now the long process of erosion could begin. The first mammals found leaves to bed down in. The first winged reptiles were trying out air currents. Dinosaurs had just set their first footprints in mud. The Rockies and other western mountain ranges waited to begin their race for the clouds. But, Mammoth Cave had already begun!

JEFF GREENBERG

Hundreds of cave entrances nestle *in the hilly landscape of Mammoth Cave National Park. White Cave, depicted here, boasts a low entrance sheltered by layered limestone.*

THE SOLUTION OF LIMESTONE

As the land rose, underground pressure buckled layer upon layer of limestone, cracking the protective sandstone caprock more and more with each passing century. Forests sprang forth from soil-covered ridgetops and animals fed on lush leaves and grasses.

Soft rains fell and, in a downward journey, picked up small amounts of carbon dioxide from the air in both sky and soil. Forming a weak solution of carbonic acid, the water encountered limestone, reacting in steps that produced calcium and bicarbonate ions. As decades progressed, so did the water. At times, the water was highly acidic, with a fast flow rate. During those times, wide cracks in the bedrock were made higher and wider. The underground streams created canyons 60 feet high and only a few feet wide.

At other times, the flow of water was almost indiscernible. Then the slow-moving water formed wide, low, elliptical passageways. The water worked on both floor and ceiling, fingering its way between bedding planes on either wall. For centuries the water worked, and underground river-dissolving limestone at its weakest joints, always moving downward.

A first level of cave appeared, and then a second. Today, Mammoth Cave has at least five known levels of interconnecting passageways. Each level boasts an intricate system of avenues. Each level connects to the one above it and below it. Most passageways are dry, but, at the deepest level visited, the river is still at work—375 feet beneath the earth's surface.

As cave explorers enter the passages of Mammoth, numerous clues hint to the flow rate of the ancient carver of rock. Streams that roared and rushed through limestone left gravel-covered floors, steep inclines, tight, meandering curves, and canyons to be traversed. Where water movement was slow and silent, floors are covered in silt and sand. The tube-shaped passages boast level floors between limestone walls that sweep and meander.

Above it all sits the sandstone. That sturdy "roof" protects the many dry and few wet passageways, shedding rainwater to vertical cracks and underground "drainpipes." The protective sandstone caprock has prevented the already formed passageways from suffering further erosion, helping to create the world's longest known cave system.

During the Mississippian Period, the southern *continent was covered by a sea. With the help of fossils, such as this horn coral embedded in the limestone wall, geologists have ascertained that the water was generally less than 50 feet deep in the Mammoth Cave area.*

CHIP CLARK

CHIP CLARK

The landscape in and around Mammoth Cave National Park is dimpled by "sinkholes," bowl-shaped depressions in fields of corn, soybeans, or tobacco. The sinks funnel rainwater and melting snow into underlying caves. Unfortunately, they sometimes send down sewage, pesticides and other pollutants as well.

CAVE HYDROLOGY

Visitors who enter Mammoth Cave National Park from the vicinity of Interstate 65 get a firsthand view of a landform known as *karst* topography. Named for a similar landform in Yugoslavia, the region is noted for specific characteristics. There are few rippling creeks or abandoned stream beds decorating the south central Kentucky landscape. Instead, bowl-shaped funnels are formed where cracks in the limestone become so widened by erosions that soil and pieces of bedrock drop into the growing chasms.

Some sinkholes are created by cave collapse. A number of sinkholes in the Mammoth Cave area are as large as several hundred feet in diameter, and more than 100 feet deep. Water can journey down through openings in the bottoms or sides of sinkholes leading directly to caves. There are so many sinkholes in the Mammoth Cave area that rainwater disappears underground long before it can create surface streams.

From the sinkhole plains visitors' drive upward, cresting the sandstone-covered ridges of the Chester Upland. Here slowly weathered sandstone caprock protects the softer limestone beneath, preserving ancient underground dry river passages.

Many people who venture into the long-abandoned river beds of Mammoth Cave have difficulty understanding the relationship between the dry passages of Mammoth and the Green River on the surface. As the Green River slowly cut through rock, the land rose to meet it in much the same way that lumber meets a stationary saw blade. Standing inside a high canyon passage during a heavy rain, many have the subconscious belief that the cave will flood from wet, roaring horizontal passages above them. Actually, the sandstone caprock sheds rainwater to the sinkhole "gutter system," where water pours down vertical shafts to the water table, 360 feet below ground.

Scattered over 53,000 acres of Mammoth Cave National Park are more than 250 cave entrances. Some of those entrances lead into the Mammoth Cave system. Most do not. A number of privately owned caves near the park have been shown commercially since the nineteenth century, and do not connect to the Mammoth Cave system. As least two privately owned "wild caves," Weller and Roppel, have been connected to Mammoth Cave in recent years. While it seem virtually impossible to connect all theses caves through exploration, hydrologists concur that all the caves in this "land of ten thousand sinks" are most likely hydrologically connected.

Of the twenty-odd entrances to Mammoth Cave, approximately one fourth are natural. The most famous of these is the historic entrance located behind the park's visitor center. Until 1921, it was the only known entrance to Mammoth Cave. Another natural entrance, Proctor Cave, was first believed to be a separate cave and was shown commercially in the mid-1800s.

Six entrances to the cave are natural entrances that have been modified in some way. Crystal Cave, located in Flint Ridge, is one of these. The 1972 connection between Crystal Cave and Mammoth Cave resulted in Mammoth's status as the world's longest cave system.

About a dozen entrances are artificial. Violet City, seen on maps at the visitor center, is one. The man-made elevator shaft used to transport supplies into the cave is also classified as an artificial entrance.

Relational boaters and motorists using the Green River ferries are often under the assumption that, since they are on the surface, Mammoth Cave

Layers of limestone shelter River Styx Spring, which flows out of Mammoth Cave and into the Green River. During periods of flooding, however, wooden gauges measure the water's rise as it reverses its flow, introducing both debris and food to the cave habitat.

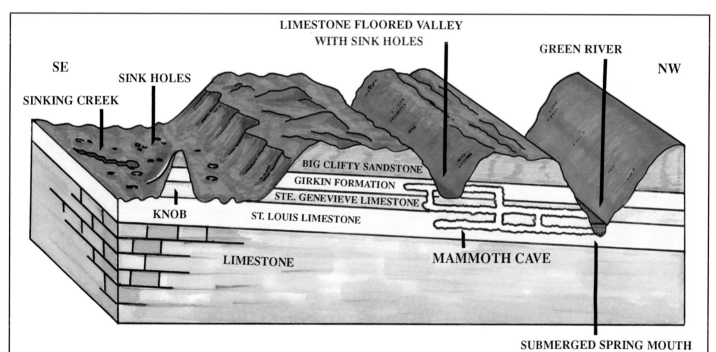

South central Kentucky boasts four key elements necessary for cave development. 1) Annual rainfall is crucial for cave formation, and Kentucky has substantial amounts. 2) The water flows down through a 'recharge area' consisting of sinking streams and sinkholes. 3) This rainfall makes its way into soluble limestone, entering thousands of openings still too small for cavers. 4) As water dissolves limestone, it creates vertical shafts and horizontal passages, often flowing many miles underground, then out of Mammoth Cave through numerous submerged springs and into the "discharge area," Green River. Unfortunately, this water too often carries pollutants.

KURT ERLANSON

While Mammoth Cave *lends its name to the national park, nearly 300 other caves are located within park boundaries. Many of them, like Blue Spring Cave, were first visited by prehistoric cultures and are considered archaeological sites. Occasionally happened upon canoeists or hikers, these caves are best left alone.*

must be entirely beneath them. In truth, the cave is not *under* them, but *above* them in the rocky cliffs on the south bank of the river. The water table in Mammoth Cave is at the same level as the Green River on the surface. Following heavy rains, the Green River floods its banks, reversing the flow of underground springs and flooding cave passages on the lowest levels. Flood waters carry numerous types of flora and fauna into the cave, "restocking the shelves" for dozens of cave species dependent upon food carried to the cave by water and surface-loving animals. When the cave's water level recedes it leaves large deposits of sand and silt.

THE NEW MADRID PROJECT

The nitrate-rich sediment in the cave resulted in the first known witnesses to earthquakes in Mammoth Cave. By 1811, a commercial saltpeter extraction had been in progress inside Mammoth Cave for several years. On December 16, 1811, a powerful sequence of earthquakes occurred along the New Madrid fault zone. This zone, 200 miles long and 40 miles wide, occurs along the axis of the Mississippi Embayment from Memphis, Tennessee, to Cairo, Illinois. It is estimated that this first earth-

"This **water** *meant* **business."**

quake would have reached a magnitude of 8.6 on the Richter Scale.

Working at leaching vats more than a quarter mile inside the cave, the saltpeter miners saw the monstrous passageway heave with dust, then heard a strong, whistling noise like hurricane winds. Those noises could have been caused by "P" waves (primary waves) moving through rock. Some rocks fell from the cave's walls and ceiling, but none of the men reported any major injuries.

Today, visitors often ask questions about the effects of the New Madrid earthquake. That same earthquake caused sections of the great Mississippi River to run backward for two days, and emitted more than 1,800 separate aftershocks during the next four months.

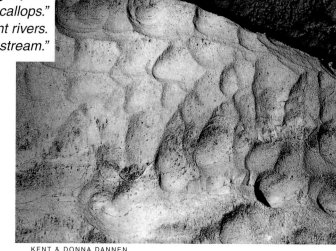

Many walls in Mammoth Cave are not rough and jagged, but are smoothly decorated with carved indentations called "scallops." The scallop's shape hints to the flow direction of the ancient rivers. The pointed edge of the scallop is headed "downstream."

KENT & DONNA DANNEN

DECORATIONS AND DEPOSITS

Visitors to Mammoth cave are often surprised buy the lack of dripstone formations. While impressed by the immense size of the high corridors boasting layer upon layer of Girkin, Ste. Genevieve, and St. Louis limestone, people cannot help by wonder why there is so few decorative deposits. All caves are formed by water. While many are created by the vertical movement of water droplets, Mammoth was not. The water that created Mammoth Cave was erosive, flowing horizontally underground. Relatively few places in the cave were obviously made by showering, slowly dripping, or vertically trickling water (although they *can* be seen in the cave). The water that developed Mammoth Cave's intricate system of passageways was not there to create delicate underground castles of fairylands. This water meant business.

For all that, the cave walls and ceilings are actually crowded with underground sculpture, decoration, and deposits. Stalactites on ceilings and stalagmites on floors are only two of many mineral deposits (speleothems) to be seen. All of the formations are the results of water interacting with bedrock.

Two of the most commonly noticed characteristics of the cave walls are *scallops* and *anastomoses* (Greek, for "an outlet, opening"). The scallops are spoon-shaped hollows dissolved in limestone floors, walls and ceilings. Caused by the flow of underground streams, the size and shape of scallops can give clues to the river's last sustained direction and rate of flow. The smaller the scallop, the faster the current.

When the Flint Ridge was connected to Mammoth Cave Ridge in 1972, Mammoth Cave's mileage jumped so dramatically that it became the world's longest cave. Keller Well, located in Flint Ridge, showcases water's adeptness as sculpting vertical crevices in limestone.

SAM FRUSHOUR

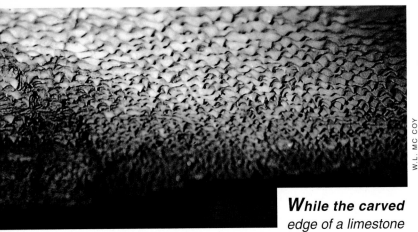

W.L. MC COY

While the carved edge of a limestone scallop marks the direction from which water came and the pointed edge denotes flow direction, the size of a scallop also has meaning. The larger the scallops, the slower the river flowed. As these small scallops prove, the rivers forming Mammoth Cave sometimes "mean business!"

The National Park Service allows the public to view a variety of cave passages considered representative of the complex cave system. Supervising tour routes helps limit recreational activity to monitored cave passages. Continuous human impact would be devastating in areas where the delicate crystals of angel hair gypsum are found.

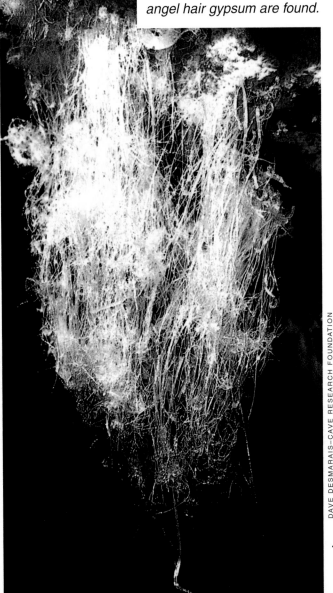

DAVE DESMARAIS—CAVE RESEARCH FOUNDATION

Anastomoses are dainty, winding tubes that interconnect in a snake-like pattern, usually along bedding plane partings. They are sometimes noticed on flat ceilings. Often confused with anastomoses, *solution pockets* are short holes located along joints in the walls or ceilings.

Travertine is a blanket geological term used for any cave formation resulting from redeposition of calcium carbonate. As water journeys down through limestone layers, it dissolves calcium carbonate, later redepositing it through precipitation. A variety of shapes are formed, depending on the behavior of the water and the physical characteristics of the passageway.

Water flowing over ledges creates *flowstone*. *Stalactites* are the result of water dripping from the ceiling, while *stalagmites* form when milky white droplets splash to the floor. The two sometimes join to make *columns*. *Helictites*, on the other hand, have a twisted, knotted shape resulting from water seeping so slowly that the thin film of calcium carbonate sticks in a haphazard fashion to the side of a speleothem without dripping off. *Cave popcorn* forms cauliflower-shaped clusters, deposited on cave walls through limestone pores, or by silvery splashes of a waterfall. *Rimstone* forms around the edges of temporary pools of calcium carbonate-laden water.

Dripstone speleothems are rare in the Mammoth Cave system. They are found where the sandstone caprock has been eroded, allowing water seepage into cave passageways.

The majority of the cave is dry, promoting the growth of *mirabilite* and *epsomite*. These small quantities of crystallized salts can form hairlike tendrils from ceilings, walls, and floors, or can have the appearance of wisps of cotton. Mirabilite and epsomite seem to form more readily in winter, disappearing as humidity increases.

Gypsum (calcium sulfate) is one of the most beautiful decorative minerals in the Mammoth Cave system. The slight amounts of water that sneak past the sandstone caprock are drawn to dry passages by capillary activity. The water then evaporates, leaving calcium minerals that grow from the base near the rock pores. Gypsum may grow in straight, swordlike needles (reaching lengths of up to 30 inches), in delicate flower shapes, tendrils, or in sheets covering walls, ceilings, or floors. Gypsum also forms in limestone cracks and fissures, as if cementing the water-worn rock. Small sheets of the snowy white gypsum will sometimes shatter to the floor, having blistered so much that it is unable to keep its growing weight tight to the ceiling.

Gypsum flowers such as those found in Mammoth Cave's "Little Paradise" were an enticing incentive to the cave's first prehistoric explorers. For 20 centuries the shimmering minerals were scraped from cave walls, yet their ancient purpose remains a mystery.

CHIP CLARK

Some cave deposits are so commonly seen that they are too often taken for granted. *Sediment* is as deep as 80 feet in some upper-level passages. Other avenues are entirely filled with bedded sand and gravel (deposited by running water), then a thin layer of silt and clay (left by ponded floodwater). Chips, slabs, and blocks of rock that have fallen from cave ceilings and walls are called *breakdown*. Numerous cave trails switchback up and over piles of breakdown as high as 90 feet. Breakdown is a normal development in the creation of caves, primarily occurring as water tables lower and cave walls and ceilings begin to dry.

What an amazing natural phenomenon Mammoth Cave is! Revered as the longest cave in the world, perhaps it should also be nominated the most stable cave known to man.

All the entrances to Mammoth Cave are nestled under a handful of ridges. If there are others, they remain hidden, providing access for bats, crickets, and other cave dwellers. Shadowed by water, ferns, or a canopy of trees, more entrances hide. Slowly they draw breath, inhaling and exhaling with each new season, quietly awaiting the first footsteps of discovery.

SUGGESTED READING

PALMER, ARTHUR N. *A Geological Guide to Mammoth Cave National Park.* New Jersey: Zephyrus Press, 1981.

PENICK, JAMES L., JR. *The New Madrid Eathquakes.* Columbia, Missouri: University of Missouri Press, 1981.

WHITE, WILLIAM B. and ELIZABETH L. WHITE. *Karst Hydrology: Concepts from the Mammoth Cave Area.* New York: Van Nostrand Reinhold, 1989.

Pools of water become saturated with calcium carbonate, depositing rimstone crusts or natural dams. These dams reach heights of three or more feet in some parts of the cave, but this one, referred to as the "Great Wall of China," is only a few inches high with a three-foot diameter. Located in the cave's "Frozen Niagara" area, the formation was first seen in 1923.

JEFF GREENBERG

*"**M**ost of the 53,000 acres of Mammoth Cave National Park were once farmland. Sixty years have changed the landscape, shading in with secondary growth, but that old sharecropper, the groundhog, remains."*

Life in the Light

These birdfoot violets, blooming on Flint Ridge Road, are named for their deeply segmented leaves, resembling the claws of a crow.

THOMAS A. SCHNEIDER

For nearly 200 years, tradition has credited Mammoth Cave's discovery to an early Kentuckian named John Houchins. Legend has it that, while hunting, Houchins shot and wounded an aging black bear, then followed the dying animal down the hillside and into the gaping entrance of Mammoth Cave.

Whether or not the details of the cave's discovery are true, the imagery painted by the story symbolizes the bigger, more important picture. The bear's pained and desperate efforts to elude Houchins in a branch crushing, dirt-and-heel downhill race represent what too often happens when man and animal compete for habitat. Sometimes, the animal wins. More often, man wins. Consistently, everyone loses.

THREATS OF SPECIES

The black bear would have been a commonly seen animal in the eighteenth and early nineteenth centuries, but is no longer found in western Kentucky. In fact, it has only been in recent years that these rulers of eastern forests have once again begun to be sighted in heavily wooded eastern portions of the state. Bison were also native. It is probable that a buffalo trail once stretched very near the historic entrance to Mammoth Cave.

The wilderness that attracted both American Indians and frontiersmen threatened them, as well.

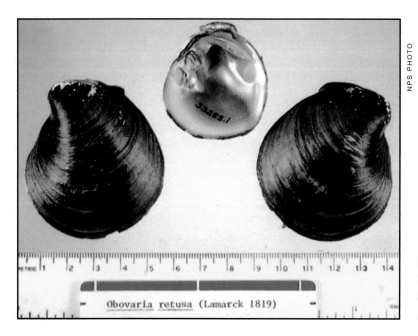

NPS PHOTO

Obovaria retusa (Lamarck 1819)

The pearled pink, gold, and aquamarine hues of freshwater mussels caused Native Americans to use them as decorative ornamentations. Misuse by commercial manufacturers later led to dangerous declines in mussel populations.

One of the park's most commonly
seen surface dwellers, a cautious
doe returns our gaze as if to remind us that we share the land with other
living beings. Be assured that baby hides nearby.

W.L. MC COY

Man's efforts to raise children, livestock, and crops in a safe environment led to greatly diminished populations of some animal species. As homes sprang up and plowed fields expanded, the land above Mammoth Cave sheltered fewer natural predators. As years slipped away, so did the gray wolf. The feared "panther," or mountain lion, all but disappeared. Beaver and muskrat were killed for their pelts. In their quest for a safe environment and financial security, pioneers and Indians both inadvertently an intentionally removed links and tied knots in the chain of life above Mammoth Cave.

AQUATIC LIFE

The Green River that runs through the park is home to numerous species of aquatic life. Sunlight filters through calcium-rich, emerald-green water and flashes on the glistening tails of catfish, bass, bluegill, and trout.

Beneath the waters of the river lies an unfamiliar animal, often overlooked. This silent creature has adapted for existence in mud, sand, and gravel. Freshwater mussels, *naiads*, are descendants of mollusks that evolved in prehistoric oceans, having begun life in the light more than 400 million years ago. Over the centuries, many species of freshwater mussels have evolved. More than 70 species of these mussels survive within the Green River of

THOMAS A. SCHNEIDER

Mischievous and noisy, the gray squirrel seems to play in every woodland scene with in the park. Seemingly carefree, this yearlong harvester is a reliable forest sentry, warning of approaching intruders.

FREDERICK D. ATWOOD

The pileated woodpecker, often spotted near the park's "Heritage Trail," boasts a red crest. Its body length rivals that of a crow!

"...skunk makes his presence known even above the smell of frying bacon."

Kentucky. Approximately two thirds of those species are found within Mammoth Cave National Park, providing nourishment for raccoons, fish, and waterfowl.

American Indians shaped mussel shells into tools and jewelry, and sometimes used crushed shells in clay pottery. Pearls form the mussels were cherished by Indians and decoratively set into cloth, on necklaces, and into bone and bear teeth.

As the nineteenth century ended, the shells were being used to manufacture pearl buttons. The industry skyrocketed until many of the mussel beds were nearly depleted. Today, these quiet animals fight to survive in their fragile environment. Brine pollution from nearby oil fields wreaked havoc on mussel populations in the 1950s and 1960s. Since then, many species have recovered, yet threats remain. Comfortable in the plankton-rich waters of sun-warmed rivers, freshwater mussels cannot survive the colder, more turbulent water released from some lakes and dams.

Most of the 53,000 acres of Mammoth Cave National Park were once farmland. Sixty years have changed the landscape, shading in with secondary growth, but that old sharecropper, the groundhog, remains.

W. L. MC COY

WILDLIFE

Some Americans associate their national parks with wildlife, hoping to see nature's children from the comfort of their own automobiles and motor homes. Visitors to Mammoth Cave National Park are no exception. And, as do her sister parks, Mammoth Cave proves no disappointment.

The cotton-white flag of the Eastern white-tailed deer is a common sight as mother and twin fawns bound into the camouflage of the forest. Both squirrels and chipmunks dance about on the woodland floor, consuming hickory nuts and acorns, occasionally covering a winter "stash" with leaves. Many of their hidden caches will be forgotten, allowing new trees to sprout and revive the forest. Campers will attest to the persistence of that pesky rascal the raccoon, and brother skunk makes his presence known even above the smell of frying bacon.

Canoeists and boaters enjoy the sight of a graceful blue heron as it glides easily above the waters of the Green River. Those same boaters know to keep an eye open for snakes as they pull

THOMAS A. SCHNEIDER

The regal American kestrel is the smallest falcon in the United States. Residing in tree cavities or cliff embankments, it feeds on insects, rodents, lizards, and small birds.

The diligent box turtle is frequently sighted near roadsides, but is also seen in and around such wet areas as Green River, Sloan's Crossing Pond, and First Creek Lake.

W.L. MC COY

The reddish-brown copperhead snake is sometimes seen by visitors. When encountered, the snakes are "relocated" to lesser-used areas where they continue to control rodent populations.

ROBERT J. CETERA

canoes up on land. Two species of poisonous snakes are found in the park. The copperhead's brownish body carries an hourglass design; it may be found near water or in old woodpiles. The timber rattlesnake boasts yellowish to blackish colorings.

Most visitors never encounter either of these pit vipers but, when it happens, the snakes are best

TOM TILL

Spring first brings the
lavender gowns of eastern
redbuds, playing the bridesmaid's role in a colorful
woodland wedding procession. Then, the forest
celebrates the arrival of hundreds of brides in snowy
white, as the dogwoods burst into bloom.

Easily identified, the down seeds of butterfly
weed were sometimes used as stuffing
instead of feathers in
cushions and beds.

ROBERT J. CETERA

W.L. MC COY

Also called "Indian turnip," the
powdered root of the Jack-in-the-pulpit
was made into flour by American Indians.

left alone. While the snakes will not win any popularity contests, they are protected within the national park. The varied reptile population found at Mammoth Cave has a right to its life in the light.

Many park animals are nocturnal and rarely seen. The best way to view the more reclusive species is to go where they are. Hikes near clearings or over river bluffs show nature at its best. An elusive fox may be glimpsed in the midst of blackberry briars. The regal wild turkeys "strut their stuff" in the cool shade of a pawpaw patch, and the red head of a pileated woodpecker dots the green-fringed forest.

THE BIG WOODS

Due to the foresight of early twentieth century Kentuckians who helped to set aside Mammoth Cave lands as a national park, one of the largest stands of virgin timber in Kentucky is protected. The Big Woods, a 300-acre old growth forest located completely within the park, is an identified remnant of the ancient forests that once covered nearly 23 million acres of Kentucky. Magnificent tulip poplar, sugar maple and American beech trees have lived on fertile, moist acres of Big Woods for centuries. Drier areas boast large stands of white oak and black oak. Dozens of trees in Big Woods are three or four feet in diameter!

KENT & DONNA DANNEN

The soft-pink hues of mountain *laurel paint a watercolored scene on shady hillsides in late spring and early summer. This flowering beauty thrives near Mammoth Cave's historic entrance.*

WILDFLOWERS

Hikes through McCoy Hollow, Raymer Hollow, and over the Green River Bluffs are colored with nature's pastels and vibrant hues. In spring, the water colored lavender and white of phlox paint the roadcuts while the brilliant red of fire pinks, snowy white trilliums, and saxifrage peek from the washes and riverbanks. Jack-in-the-pulpit reads his devotions in bowl-shaped sinks. Bright yellow jonquils stream like sunshine down the hillsides and dwarf irises kneel, tiny fairies cloaked in royal purple, on the forest floor.

Summer brings the lacy beauty of mountain laurel, pink wild roses, and blue chicory. Along with the bountiful greens of mints, ferns, honeysuckle, and blackberry, they stand in glorious tribute to life in the light.

SUGGESTED READING

ANGIER, BRADFORD. *Field Guide to Medicinal Plants.* Harrisburg, Pennsylvania: Stackpole, Books, 1978.

WHARTON, MARY E. and ROGER W. BARBOUR. *The Wildflowers of Kentucky.* Lexington, Kentucky: University Press of Kentucky, 1971.

JEFF GNASS

The morning sun finds autumn hardwoods *and warms the ridgetops over hundreds of caves. Early logging industry brought the felling of thousands of trees in the Mammoth Cave area. Hardwoods furnished flooring, ship's masts, railroad ties, and fine woodworking pieces. Farmers split logs to make rail fences, shingles, stove wood, and tobacco sticks.*

Overleaf : *Tour boat on Green River Photo by Chip Clark*

*"**D**eep in the cave's lowest level live species who have reluctantly sacrificed habitat mobility. Trapped in the cave between glacial advances more than ten thousand years ago..."*

Life in the Dark

Within the cave, darkness prevails. And, for centuries, progression of human culture has resulted in various methods of cave lighting. The energy crisis of the early 1970s brought the use of fluorescent lighting. Used only recently on the most frequently traveled tour routes, fluorescent fixtures have greatly impacted the cave.

While ferns do perch on interior walls at cave entrances, passages beyond the "twilight zone" should naturally be void of green plant life. Sunlight is needed for the different phases of photosynthesis to occur. Mammoth Cave has no light penetration beyond the entrances. Use of fluorescent lighting, however, creates a "scattering" of light on walls that promotes the growth of various species of green and blue algae and mosses. In rare instances, ferns can be seen growing in cave soil near light fixtures more than one-half mile inside the cave!

Roots from these growing plants cause soil disturbance and mar cave walls. In areas where dripstone formations are found, the spreading algae becomes saturated with water as moisture enters the cave, causing calcium-laden water droplets to neither make new formations nor add to older ones.

Park officials are attempting to correct imbalances caused by fluorescent lights. As time and money permit, old fixtures are replaced by low wattage incandescent bulbs and directed away from cave walls when possible. Growing patches of algae are then cleaned from cave walls. In the meantime, the plants create an unnatural food source for many cave animals.

Natural history has predetermined the coloration within Mammoth Cave. Red, beige, and butterscotch-orange are typical of all caves in the region. Mammoth Cave does, however, boast two colors that most do not: fluorescent lighting has caused both green and blue algae to thrive on some cave walls.

KENT & DONNA DANNEN

CHIP CLARK

Nineteenth-century guides developed a method of lighting trails that was unique to Mammoth Cave. Handcrafting their own props from slender pieces of hickory, oak, walnut, or ash, they used their "torch sticks" to throw burning twists of fuel-soaked rags into the darker regions of large rooms, deep pits, and high domes. This cave illumination technique continued through 1990.

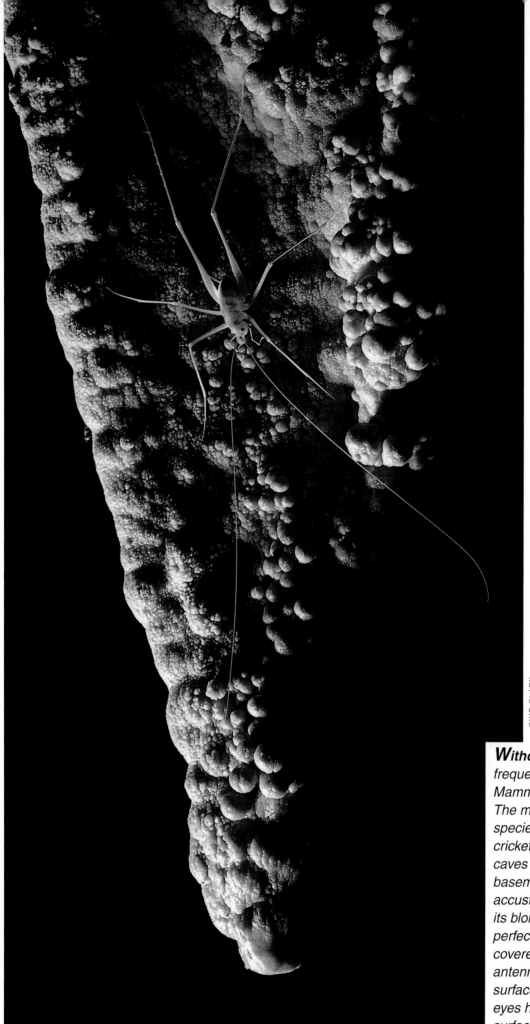

CHIP CLARK

"...thousands of bats seek shelter within Mammoth Cave..."

Without a doubt, the most frequently seen animal in Mammoth Cave is the cricket. The most prominent of these is a species called the "camelback cricket," an insect found in many caves and, sometimes, in basements. This cricket is accustomed to the darkness and its blonde coloration gives it perfect camouflage on dust-covered limestone walls. Slender antennae make long trips to the surface easier. Once topside, eyes help it make selections at a surface "salad bar."

CONNIE TOOPS

CONNIE TOOPS

Bats are the only major predator of night-flying insects. The big brown bat (above) *can eat up to 3,000 insects a night. Making up approximately 25 percent of all mammals, bats—like dolphins—communicate and navigate with high-frequency sounds. The eastern pipistrel (right) can detect obstacles as fine as human hair.*

One of the most commonly seen cave animals is the cave cricket. This cricket survives both in the cave and on the surface. Even in Mammoth Cave the food chain ultimately begins with plants. Under normal conditions, animals like the cave cricket journey outside for food. Unnatural growth of green plants inside the cave can cause some animals to "jump at opportunity." Instead of using their long antennae and legs to find their way up vertical shafts to dine in a surface "salad bowl," they opt for that more easily obtained algae and mosses.

Cave crickets are usually blonde in color. They use their eyesight when visiting the surface. Several species of crickets can be found on all cave tour routes, but are seen in greatest numbers at the New Entrance or at Rainbow Dome.

While the cave temperature (54°- 57°F) is too cool for snakes, other animals may be seen at cave entrances. Though rarely spotted, pack rats build nests and give birth to young just inside the cave. A variety of salamanders love the dark, moist cave. They also have a grand affection for cave crickets. Several spiders, like the orb weaver, construct webs underground and trap an occasional mosquito or cricket.

More than 30 species of animals are frequently seen inside Mammoth Cave. But, don't be fooled by the seemingly sterile, quiet darkness—more than 100 species utilize the cave's environment!

BATS

Throughout the year, as many as 12 species of bats visit the caves within Mammoth Cave National Park. Some species winter in areas nearer the equator. Others opt for hibernation within caves or barn rafters. While thousands of bats seek shelter within Mammoth Cave, they are rarely seen on tour routes. During hibernation, some species like to sleep in the cold air breathed through natural cave openings. Others, like the pipistrel, prefer the high humidity found deeper in the cave.

With few exceptions, bats at Mammoth Cave National Park are small and have a wingspan of seven or eight inches. Feeding on mosquitoes, moths, and other flying insects, females give single births once every one or two years. A bat's heart

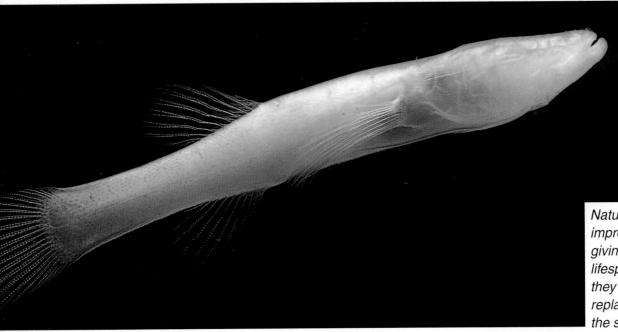

CHIP CLARK

Unpredictable food availability strengthens odds against successful reproduction in eyeless cave fish. Natural evolution has improved the odds by giving the animals a long lifespan. After many tries, they may successfully replace only themselves in the species population.

While some cave dwellers simply choose to enjoy the damp, cool underground environment, other animals, like this isopod, have evolved to the point that they could not survive outside the cave.

CHIP CLARK

may beat hundreds of times in one minute during a frenzied evening of feeding. Yet, its heart may slow to a single beat every few minutes during hibernation.

Bats are not fond of noise and light encountered on the tour trails. They use their echolocation to find quieter sanctuaries in the darkness. In fact, the endangered Indiana and gray bats are protected in the park. Dixon and Colossal caves, known refuges for species, are "off limits" to human activity during hibernation periods.

THE CAVE DWELLERS

Deep in the cave's lowest level live species who have reluctantly sacrificed habitat mobility. Trapped in the cave between glacial advances more than ten thousand years ago, each new generation

This tiny, eyeless amphipod bears witness to the benefits of "getting off the interstate." Its metabolic rate is estimated to be five to ten times lower than that of its surface counterpart.

CHIP CLARK

Resembling a tiny string of seed pearls, an eyeless millipede slowly, but diligently, makes its way through Mammoth Cave. Over centuries, the millipede has genetically phased out development of eyes and coloration. Sight is of little use in complete darkness, and camouflage certainly serves no purpose here. When viewed in moderate light, such nonpigmented animals appear translucent.

CHIP CLARK

progressively adapted to the temperatures and darkness. Gradually, they lost functional eyes and coloration.

The most famous blindfish, *Amblyopsis spelaea*, appears translucent, is eyeless, and would easily fit in a person's, hand. These fish, along with blind, colorless crayfish, live a slow, seemingly passive lifestyle. Intent upon conserving energy, the small animals glide easily through the cave pools awaiting floodwaters that carry new food to their fragile environment.

Eyeless fish, crayfish, and freshwater Kentucky cave shrimp live years longer than their surface counterparts. This longevity increases their chances for successful reproduction.

Rarely seen by park ranges or visitors, the reclusive animals easily detect movement. Gliding beneath rock ledges or into deeper water, these true "cave dwellers" deal with floods, cave pooling due to lock and dam construction, human curiosity, and cave waterway pollution. Our ever popular, "always asked about" cave inhabitants wage an unending battle 360 feet below ground.

They compete for life in the darkness.

CHIP CLARK

The approximate size of your thumbnail, this eyeless Kentucky cave shrimp bears a marked resemblance to a "shrimp" ring found in a jewelry store. This shrimp is more valued, however, for its species is endangered. Groundwater contaminants from sinkholes, accidental toxic spills, sewage, and agricultural sources threaten this delicate animal.

SUGGESTED READING

CULVER, DAVID C. *Cave Life: Evolution and Ecology.* Cambridge, Massachusetts: Harvard University Press, 1982.

MOHR, CHARLES E. *The World of the Bat.* New York: J.B. Lippincott Co., 1976.

WAGONER, JOHN J. and LEWIS D. CUTLIFF. *Mammoth Cave.* Flagstaff, Arizona: Interpretive Publications, Inc., 1985.

"The most famous cave "mummy" found in Mammoth Cave National Park was discovered in 1935 by two cave guides. Nicknamed "Lost John," archaeologists believe he accidentally lost his life inside the cave about the year 17 B.C."

Those Who Came Before...

When a park ranger smilingly asks a child who discovered Mammoth Cave, he or she may answer, "Indians," or "people." Some children will respond with "the first one to get there." All the answers are correct, and the "first one to get there" arrived 40 centuries ago.

THE PALEO-INDIANS

More than 12,000 years ago, the landscape shook with the heavy footsteps of huge bison, giant sloths, and mastodons. Great sheets of thick glacial ice covered major portions of North America, and the forests were green with spruce, fir, and pine. Small groups of nomadic people trekked the hills and flatlands of an ever-changing "home," searching for large animals (megafauna) needed for food.

Their hands were skilled at working stone to make spear points for the hunt. They gathered nature's bounty as it made itself available, picking

THOMAS A. SCHNEIDER

Water passes through hundreds of cracks in the ceilings of mammoth Cave. Depending on the water's speed, it will either erode the limestone and widen vertical domes and pits, or redeposit rock in nature's patient manner. Park rangers frequently drop to the child's point of view when discussing the existence of groundwater and threats made upon it by our own surface pollutants.

RICH CALDWELL

The eastern wild turkey has been favored by hunters for centuries. This track, carefully placed in a sparkling powder of snow, attests to the presence of a truly impressive bird.

CHIP CLARK

***Standing dwarfed between wide**
walls and a lofty ceiling, even a human
silhouette seems to solidly resound in silent chambers.*

berries, collecting nuts and other foods throughout the year. As the moon and stars moved, so did they, traveling with the seasons to where the food was ripe. They followed the herds, too, camping for short periods of time, moving often.

As time passed, the glaciers retreated with the onset of warmer temperatures. The large bison, great mastodons, and giant ground sloths disappeared. With their extinction over time, the Paleo-Indian ("ancient Indians") learned to hunt smaller game. Their stone tools were shaped and sized for turkey, deer, or raccoon. The lush forests of a colder climate relinquished dominance to oak and hickory.

Human population increased as women gave birth to children whose eyes would never rest on the steaming body of the mastodon. After 3,000 years of hunting and gathering, the land gradually eased change upon man.

The Archaic Indians

The Archaic period is generally dated from 8000 B.C. to 1000 B.C. These people, hunters and gatherers like their ancestors, continued to grow in number. They traveled in "bands" made up of immediate family, grandparents, aunts, uncles, and in-laws, changing camp with the seasons.

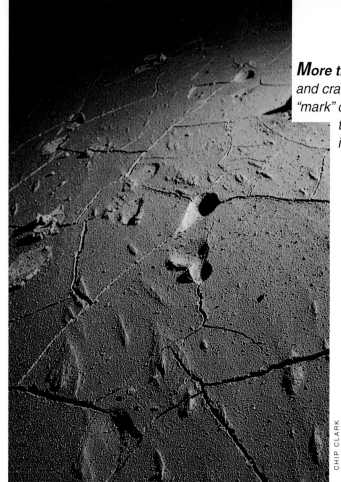

CHIP CLARK

More than once, modern cavers have squirmed, climbed, and crawled through mud and over rocks only to discover the "mark" of previous explorers. Aboriginal footprints are scattered through several caves in the park. These impressions, set in mud or sand, have remained unaltered centuries later.

As population increased, the territory of each band decreased. To survive this natural limitation, the bands became "specialized," learning to live with what their territory provided. The bands occasionally came together for socializing and trading. This contact gave them the opportunity to acquire mates, and to exchange such items as copper, cherts, and shells. Having used the entrance to Mammoth Cave as shelter for years, it was a member of a Late Archaic band who was "the first to get there," braving the mystery of Mammoth Cave to begin a 4,000-year-old legacy in the darkness.

FOOTPRINTS IN THE SAND

Because of man's growing knowledge of crop cultivation and pottery making during the years 1000 B.C. to A.D. 900, that time span has been called the "Woodland period." While they continued to hunt and gather, the Early Woodland people also grew such plants as goosefoot, sumpweed, sunflower, and maygrass. Many of these foods were carried with them on trips deep inside Mammoth Cave.

We do not know what name they might have had for this mystical chasm underground, but we do know that it was of value to them. They traversed hazardous cave terrain in search of such minerals as gypsum, epsomite, mirabilite, and selenite. No one knows for certain why they were willing to risk their lives for these deposits, but it is highly probable that the minerals were believed to be magical or to have medicinal properties. These reasons alone would have made them profitable in trade for food, shells, and other necessities or luxuries.

Contemporary cave visitors frequently inquire about cave "mummies." Several bodies of early cave users have been found in Mammoth Cave and other caves nearby. Many were found and destroyed in the last century, before proper documentation could be made.

The most famous cave "mummy" found in Mammoth Cave National Park was discovered in 1935 by two cave guides. Nicknamed "Lost John," archaeologists believe he accidentally lost his life inside the cave about the year 17 B.C. In life, this cave explorer stood 5 feet 3 inches tall, weighed 145 pounds; and was approximately 45 years old. He died *two miles* inside the cave, the breath squeezed from him by the weight of a 6.5-ton rock. Was he in search of the "hereafter" or the underworld? Was he a caving novice, or did he have a lifelong reputation as a dependable supplier of the "mystery crystals"?

Some scientists believe that the Early Woodland people had use of more than the natural entrances familiar today. They base their opinions on such studies as the 1968 discovery of skeletal bat remains near Mammoth Cave's "Chief City," two miles inside the entrance. The Brazilian freetail discovered normally would not locate that far inside of an entrance.

During the Middle Woodland period (200 B.C. to A.D. 500) rockshelter occupancy diminished. More months were spent cultivating crops on the floodplain areas. The Woodland people ceased their mineral mining and became seemingly disinterested in the physical properties of Mammoth Cave. But, so many mysteries remained! Way up high in the dust-covered ledges of Mammoth rest footprints in the sand, time-protected signatures of the "first ones to get there."

SAM FRUSHOUR

Archaeological evidence points to the conclusion that *prehistoric people mined salts, such as mirabilite, from cave walls. Mirabilite may grow in hairline tendrils, cottony tufts, or in massive flower or stalactitic shapes.*

" ...minerals were **believed** *to be* **magical** *or to have medicinal* **properties. "**

Hundreds of fragments of aboriginal slippers *(sandals) have been found in caves within the park. Fashioned between 2,000 and 4,000 years ago, the slippers were often twined in a chevron pattern, or simply twisted in an over-one-under-one design. Some favorite twining materials were cattail, hemp, grass, basswood, or paw paw inner bark, and leaves of rattlesnake-master.*

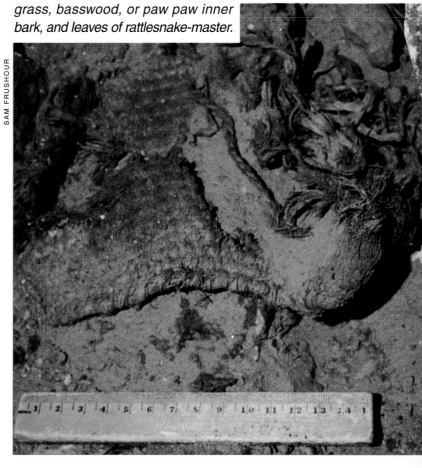

SAM FRUSHOUR

EIGHTEENTH-CENTURY IMPACT

By the eighteenth century there were few, if any, permanent residents in most of Kentucky (then part of Virginia). The Shawnee, Cherokee, and other groups used the land as a hunting ground.

During the French and Indian War of the 1750s a British soldier by the name of Thomas Hutchins was probably the first European to have reached the Mammoth Cave area. After the French were defeated, the British quickly officially proclaimed the land west of the Appalachian Mountains and south of the Ohio River an Indian reservation. Almost immediately, however, British hunters and traders began "sizing up" the Indian lands for profit. As men like Daniel Boone, John Finley, James Harrod, and other frontiersmen grew familiar with Kentucky's great natural wealth, a particular fondness for the saltpeter-rich caves developed. They needed the saltpeter to produce gunpowder and preserve meats.

The rediscovery of Mammoth Cave is not all that important—it was probably no big deal to the discoverer. To him, Mammoth Cave was just another hole in the ground. What he liked was the rich saltpeter dirt that kept the rifle hot and the venison dried.

The first "official" owner of Mammoth Cave was Valentine Simons, who claimed 200 acres, including both Mammoth and Dixon caves, in 1798, The cave was later sold to the McClean brothers and, still later, to Charles Wilkins and Fleming Gatewood. The McClean brothers began commercial production of saltpeter at Mammoth Cave, but it was the 1810 Wilkins-Gatewood purchase that really got the ball rolling.

Prior to purchasing Mammoth Cave, Wilkins had established himself as a saltpeter merchant in Louisville and Lexington. He found it profitable to supply the steadily growing Dupont gunpowder works of Delaware with rich saltpeter from Kentucky's caves.

Both Wilkins and Gatewood were excited by the promise Mammoth showed as a petre cave. They were elated by the prospect of a dependable nitrate source, and felt sure their recent purchase would prove lucrative. Relations between the United States and Britain had been shaky since the Revolution, and signs pointed to a renewal of hostility. Saltpeter sold for under $0.20 per pound in 1810. The War of 1812 resulted in a substantial price increase for gunpowder and its ingredients. By 1813, saltpeter was being purchased for $0.75 and $1 per pound.

Saltpeter production was quite extensive at Mammoth Cave, increasing steadily as the war progressed. As many as 70 slaves worked the operation, building more leaching vats and hauling dirt from distant cave areas to leaching vat locations.

Production records maintained by Charles Wilkins suggest that half of the saltpeter produced in Warren County, Kentucky, in 1812 came from Mammoth Cave. Fleming Gatewood sold his interest in Mammoth Cave soon after the war began. Wilkins and his new partner, Hyman Gratz, owned and operated both Mammoth and Dixon caves until the conflict's end in 1815. By that year, the estate had expanded from the 200 acres owned by Valentine Simons to about 2,000 acres.

With the end of the War of 1812, the price of saltpeter plummeted. But the fame of Mammoth Cave was spreading. Numerous newspaper articles described the cave's contribution to the war effort,

These saltpeter vats, located in mammoth's "Main Cave" passage, have witnessed several important events since their early nineteenth-century construction. It was here that the slave miners and others felt the effects of the New Madrid Earthquakes in 1811-12.

CHIP CLARK

Standing in this passage called "The Church," it is easy to view the effects of both natural and cultural history. Water-carved walls sweep wide around remnants of wooden waterlines, 160 feet underground. In the early 1800s, tall tulip poplar and oak trees were first cut into lengths, then hand-bored to create pipes.

CHIP CLARK

and discussed the discoveries of natural wonders and Indian "mummies" in Mammoth Cave and other caves close by. Soon, people flocked from the East to this "western frontier" to behold the marvels firsthand. Mammoth's reputation as a tourist attraction was beginning.

The Civil War brought unrest to south central Kentucky, but Mammoth Cave's saltpeter history was not reborn. The manager of the cave, a unionist, continued to conduct cave tours throughout the war years. While the Confederacy was mining saltpeter from caves in other southern states, the Union forces ware not suffering such shortages. Stories passed down through history depict chance encounters between southern and northern soldiers, each taking a moment from a saddened, hectic life to marvel at the earth's wonders in the quiet safety of Kentucky's underground.

NINETEENTH-CENTURY CAVE TOURS

With the death of Charles Wilkins in 1828, Hyman Gratz continued showing Mammoth Cave to anyone wiling to travel long distances to see it. Gratz used experienced veterans of the mining operation to escort curious travelers through wondrous passageways. Archibald Miller, an overseer from saltpeter mining days, let small groups of

amazed novices over the craggy piles of limestone rock and around hundreds of mounds of lixiviated cave dirt to view the darkness of Mammoth.

Originally called Flatt's Cave, the name had gradually changed to "Mammoth Cave," by the time the War of 1812 had started. The "Rotunda," the first large room entered, prompted the name. To the first cave visitors, the name must certainly have seemed appropriate. The walls appeared to hover! The ceilings were swallowed by darkness! And the silence—the silence hinted of the tomb.

At first, men like "Archie" Miler showed only those passages and avenues with which they were familiar. Then, as the guides grew more comfortable with the cave and fond of the attentiveness granted them by visitors, they became less hesitant. Travelers were led beyond the saltpeter areas and up into "Haunted Chambers." They risked the perils of wet, rocky floors and yawning chasms to see "Bottomless Pit" and "Crevice Pit." Curious human eyes watched in amazement as the hundreds of tiny, brown bats huddled in "Little Bat Avenue" wiped their faces and ears with folded wings only two feet above them.

As the century progressed, so did Mammoth Cave's fame. Guides began to boast of the cave's never-ending passages and, before long, newspapers proclaimed the cave more than 100 miles long. Word of mouth, combined with the publication of numerous travelogues and "first person" accounts, brought people from all over the world to the cave. Jenny Lind, Edwin Booth, Charles Dickens, Ole Bull, and Ralph Waldo Emerson visited, as did Prince Alexis of Russia, and Dom Pedro of Brazil. People from all walks of life, of various occupations, and numerous countries braved the forbidding stillness of the cave. Each was awed by it.

Throughout the 1800s, a variety of lights were used in the cave. Early visitors carried open-flame lanterns fueled by refined lard oil, but found the shadow-casting lights to be lacking. Guides ignited oiled paper to show of the large rooms, deep pits, and lofty domes. They placed burning rags on ledges and, later in the century, began throwing oil-soaked twisted rags into the darkest chasms to light their way.

Nineteenth-century visitors grew fond of the habit of smoking their names on smooth, white cave ceilings. Today, there are areas where the ceilings are covered with names, carefully scripted in soot, of visitors who walked the cave's passages more than 100 years ago.

Through trial and error, a caving costume was designed to protect the costly clothing of the cave's highly valued customers. Visitors could, for a fee, opt to wear a mustard-yellow flannel costume in to the cave to protect their traveling clothes from smoke and dust. What a spectacle they must have made, lanterns in hands, dust capes on heads, as they filed into Mammoth's yawning entrance!

EARLY GUIDES

Mammoth Cave had many early guides, but they were not compulsive cave explorers until the family of Hayman Gratz sold his caves and surface acreage to Franklin Gorin in 1838. Gorin, a prominent lawyer in Glasgow, Kentucky, had probably acquired Stephen Bishop, a young slave, his brother David, and their mother from Lowry Bishop, also of Glasgow.

Stephen Bishop was only 16 years old when he came to Mammoth Cave, but he was destined to live the rest of his life in and above the cave's passageways. Gorin acquired the brothers Mat and Nick Bransford, also slaves, from Thomas Bransford of Glasgow. Together, these three young cave guide explorers enriched and inspired black heritage rivaling that of any other National Park Service area.

Stephen was fist to cross Bottomless Pit, opening many more miles of cave. He discovered the cave's underground river system and the strange, ghost-like, eyeless animals within the water. Mat and Nick also made numerous underground discoveries, guiding cave tours until the 1870s. With their arrival at Mammoth Cave in 1838, the Bransford brothers began a 101-year Bransford guiding tradition.

Other guides, too, began "family traditions" at Mammoth Cave. Archibald Miller, Jr., followed in his father's footsteps. Fleming Gatewood's son, George, held church services 160 feet below

CHIP CLARK

"Register Hall" in "Gothic Avenue," is an extreme example of nineteenth-century visitor impact. By the 1880s, candle writing was frowned upon, but visitors soon found another way of "leaving their mark." Hundreds of monuments, like the "Kentucky Monument," pictured, were constructed by both guides and visitors.

THE NELSON COLLECTION

Will Bransford spent his life at Mammoth Cave, and represented the second of five generations of Bransfords who guided cave tours. Behind Bransford is fellow guide, Ed Bishop (circa 1902).

THE NELSON COLLECTION

Ed Bishop greatly extended the known boundaries of Mammoth Cave. A popular guide and competent caver, Ed left the area in 1917 and died in Indianapolis.

> "*He discovered...strange, ghost-like, eyeless animals within the water.*"

ground. Will Garvin married Nick Branford's daughter, Hanna, and discovered a vertical crevice called the "Corkscrew" around 1870. Joshua Wilson was the first of three generations of his family at Mammoth Cave. The Merediths, Demunbruns, Cutliffs, Livelys, Nelsons, and Frances—all these and more have greatly added to the culturally rich guiding tradition at Mammoth Cave.

With the end of the Civil War, some ex-slaves in the Mammoth Cave community left to find new homes. Others, like the Bransfords, chose to stay. Stephen Bishop died shortly before 1860, but his wife, Charlotte, and son, Thomas, still called Mammoth Cave home. Another Bishop left his mark—short, stocky Ed Bishop, mustached and muscular, was one of the finest cave guide explorers Mammoth Cave has ever produced.

Accompanied by German cartographer Max Kaemper, Ed climbed, squirmed, and wiggled through breakdown and dirt to penetrate what had previously been perceived as "the end" of Mammoth Cave. The exploration, together with the map completed by Ed Bishop and Max Kaemper in 1908 remain some of the most important accomplishments in Mammoth Cave's history.

Today, cavers covered in dust and grimy with sweat stop and gaze in reverent comradeship at the names "Stephen," "Ed Bishop," or "Nick the guide"

sooted in silent, sleeping letters on the time-worn walls of Mammoth Cave.

THE GROGHANS OF LOCUST GROVE

John Croghan (Cron) spent his childhood hiking the wooded countrysides of northern Kentucky, fishing in the Ohio River, and running footraces with his five younger brothers. He spent summer nights on the back porch of his parents' large brick home, listening to stories of faraway places—his grandparents' old home in Ireland, the thrilling grandeur of the American northwest. He tucked away the stories for savoring as he grew, knowing that someday he, too, would be a pathfinder and trailblazer, like his mother's brothers who delighted so in filling his head with dreams.

William Croghan and his wife, Lucy Clark Croghan, built their impressive brick home, "Locust Grove," in 1790 on what was then rural acreage near Louisville. Their first child, John, was born that year. When John was 27, his story-telling uncle died at Locust Grove. Dignitaries from across the state came to bid farewell to that adventurous trailblazer, George Rogers Clark.

CHIP CLARK

COURTESY LOCUST GROVE HISTORIC HOME

Several years after purchasing Mammoth Cave, Dr. John Croghan (above), a prominent Louisville physician, began an underground effort to slow the fate of more than a dozen tuberculosis suffers. Several stone and wood "consumptive huts," such as the one shown on the left were constructed for his patients. The cave's environment proved unsuitable, however, the hospital was short-lived. The soot-covered walls in the area of the "Acute Angle" remind us of his efforts.

In 1839, after touring abroad, John Croghan returned home and visited Mammoth Cave. He walked the winding passages with his guide, Archibald Miller, Jr., and was overwhelmed by the size of the rooms and avenues. Having spent numerous days at resorts for the wealthy, he agreed with Mr. Gorin's plan for improving accommodations and promoting the cave. In fact, why produce accommodations only *above* the cave? Why not build a fine hotel several miles underground, with a carriage road, library, dining hall, and ballroom! John's mind raced with possibilities as he heard opportunity knocking.

Always ready to take a risk (he struck Kentucky's first oil in Cumberland County in 1829) Croghan offered Franklin Gorin $10,000 for his Mammoth Cave property. Hesitantly, Gorin accepted his offer, handing over the allegiance of Stephen, Mat and Nick, as well.

Under Croghan's ownership, Mammoth Cave began to flourish. He paid extensive advertisements, called in numerous favors, and put plenty of hammers, nails, and carpenters to use. His spacious Mammoth Cave Hotel served visitors from all over

the world until its destruction by fire in 1916.

A practicing physician since 1814, Doctor John Croghan had earned his medical degree from the University of Pennsylvania. Thus, he looked at the cave from a medical viewpoint as well. He had read of underground consumption hospitals while in Europe, and felt that Mammoth Cave might help in the search of a cure for tuberculosis. He and other physicians concluded that the moist air and constant temperature of the cave might quiet the rages of that dreaded disease.

In 1842, Doctor Croghan had Stephen and the Bransfords construct both stone and wood huts within the cave, then invited as many as 15 tuberculosis patients to participate in the experiment. The underground consumptive hospital proved a failure, but two stone huts and heavily blackened cave walls remain as reminders of his medical efforts. Several of the patients who died at Mammoth Cave are buried in the Old Guide's Cemetery near the cave entrance. There cave guide Stephen Bishop rests also.

Croghan contracted tuberculosis and died in 1849, after several years of ill health, a bachelor, he left the Mammoth Cave estate in trusteeship for his nieces and nephews. The doctor's death began more than 70 years of lessees and resident managers at Mammoth Cave. Oddly enough it was the beginning of a legacy.

John Croghan's nieces and nephews who inherited the Mammoth Cave Estate lived in various cities across the country and chose to employ managers for their uncle's holdings.

Each subsequent lessee and manager affected the reputation of Mammoth Cave. Larkin J. Procter, who resided near Bell's Tavern, managed the cave in the late 1850s. Upon the expiration of Procter's lease, E. K. Owsley and his brother, John, managed the cave through the Civil War years. The war proved especially unfortunate for the Owsleys. While their cave guides, accommodations, and meals were widely lauded, the resort business was far from profitable. Their years at Mammoth Cave were further shrouded by the death of E. K. Owsley's young son, who was fatally burned when a string of firecrackers draped over his shoulder accidentally ignited.

Following the Civil War, travel to Mammoth Cave substantially decreased. In the 1870s, Dave L. Graves of Lebanon, Kentucky, leased the cave. Strikingly tall, with a head for business, he immediately made much needed improvements to the grounds and cave trails. Advertising extensively, he prompted renewed visitation to Mammoth Cave. Year's later, friends would remember him as a progressive man of strong character. They bragged that he set a good table, kept a good bar, and employed a good group of guides and waiters. But, most impressive to some, were the billiard hall and two billiard tables he provided for entertainment.

Graves left Mammoth Cave following legal disputes with a competitive stageline and the Mammoth Cave trustees. Both disputes were settled in Graves' favor.

The following years brought Francis Klett and his underground mushroom farm. They also brought W. C. Comstock, an enterprising man who initiated the Mammoth Cave Railroad.

Manager Henry C. Ganter accompanied Mammoth Cave to the twentieth century, During Ganter's stay, numerous photographs were made of the cave. These black and white depictions provide a valuable record of a Victorian era in Kentucky.

JEFF GREENBAUM

Visitors sometimes travel a winding path from the park's "Heritage Trail," and find themselves at Mammoth Dome Sink. Laced with a variety of ferns and shrouded by paw paw trees, this more famous sinkhole shoots water into an underlying crevice. Once the water enters the cave, it falls 192 feet to the historic trail in Mammoth Cave.

For more than 160 years, visitors have been drawn to the echoing enchantment of the cave's youngest passages. Echo River is one of nearly 20 known rivers in Mammoth Cave.

PHOTO BY ROBERT J. CETERA

Mammoth Cave Gains World Attention

The twentieth century did not dawn quietly in the Mammoth Cave community. The 1870s rivalry between David Graves' stageline and that of Andy McCoy had begun an unhealthy competitiveness that raged well into the 1900s. As cave tourism seemed more obviously "here to stay," local landowners found it profitable to show their caves to Mammoth Cave travelers.

Diamond Cave, located between Bell's Tavern and Mammoth Cave, had been shown since the mid-1800s, and was noted for its dripstone formations. Procter Cave, between Diamond and Mammoth, was most heavily visited in the decades following the Civil War. Both Dossey and Ganter caves, overlooking the Green River, were promoted. Colossal, Great Onyx, and Floyd Collins' Crystal Cave were popular tour caves located under nearby Flint Ridge.

Colossal Cave was, as its name suggests, noted for its spacious rooms. Great Onyx boasted delicate dripstone formations, including helictites. The walls of Crystal Cave glistened with various gypsum minerals, some spiraling from the wall and measuring more than 12 inches in length.

DEATH OF A CAVER

Days in south central Kentucky slipped by unnoticed by the rest of the world. Families eked a living by logging poplar, oak, and walnut to craft furniture and board-feet lumber. Before 1931, the twentieth century saw steamboat travel on the Green River, but it took the death of Floyd Collins in 1925, to place worldwide attention on Mammoth Cave.

Floyd Collins, an avid caver and part owner of Crystal Cave, became the subject of a media blitz in 1925. Trapped in nearby Sand Cave on January 30, Floyd began a two-week ordeal that was destined to be forever recorded in both Mammoth Cave and Kentucky history. Readers and listeners all over the

country kept up on rescue attempts to free Floyd from the tight crawlway and watermelon-sized rock that pinned his legs and held him captive. News coverage and commercial exploitation of Collins' tragic accident and subsequent death brought nationwide attention to the Mammoth Cave area of Kentucky.

A NATIONAL PARK IS BORN

The year before Floyd's death, the Mammoth Cave National Park Association was formed by both Kentucky businessmen and politicians in an effort to establish Mammoth Cave as a national park. As early as 1911, efforts had been made to create a national park in Kentucky. Congress had repeatedly responded that "just a cave" was not enough.

Concerned citizens made Congress aware of the spectacular scenery and cultural history *above* the cave. They reminded Congress of the area's rivers that were so important to eastern transportation and commerce, connecting the colonies to what

*E*stablished in 1827, the Mammoth Cave Baptist *Church is one of three church buildings still standing within the park. There are more than seventy cemeteries in Mammoth Cave National Park, and park officials maintain cemetery listings used by family members and genealogists. Located on the winding Flint Ridge Road, this church cemetery contains the grave of Floyd Collins, a caver who died in nearby Sand Cave in 1925. Joppa Baptist Church and Cemetery, Highway 70 West, and Good Spring Baptist Church and Cemetery, located north of Green River, are also quiet retreats.*

ROBERT J. CETERA

CHIP CLARK

The Wild Cave Tour
*gives visitors a chance
to see areas "off the beaten path," like
this gypsum encrusted passage.*

was once "wilderness." Because of their commercial and cultural importance, Nolin River, Green River, and Bylew Creek were proposed for inclusion.

Some farsighted people believed that many of the local caves could be interconnected, and that the park should be large enough to protect *all* the caves. While their thinking was sound and their hearts resolute, even they never dreamed the cave would prove to be as extensive as we know it to be, today stretching beyond park boundaries and beneath private lands. Worldwide concern over the Floyd Collins' incident, coupled with energetic efforts of the association, resulted in passage of legislation that officially authorized the preparation of Mammoth Cave as a national park in 1926.

Although Congress established Mammoth Cave as our 26th national park in 1926, it was not made "official" until President Franklin D. Roosevelt put pen to paper on July 1, 1941. The unfortunate dawning of World War II postponed a dedication ceremony until September, 1946.

In a region of rolling hills and lengthy wagon rides, *the turn-of-the-century runs of a little train called "Hercules," brought both visitors and dry goods from Glasgow Junction (Park City) to Mammoth Cave.*

THE JIM CARROLL COLLECTION–PHOTO BY ROBERT J. CETERA

Mammoth Cave National Park offers diverse activities for people of various ages and physical capabilities. One such tour, affectionately dubbed "Trog" (short for troglodyte meaning cave dweller) by park rangers, is an opportunity for children aged 8 through 12 to broaden their knowledge of our environment. Several different cave routes may be used for this "kids only" activity. This youngster pauses momentarily to catch his breath in White Cave, located near the headquarters campground.

ROBERT J. CETERA

National Park Service personnel perform a varied range of duties. While interpretation of our natural and cultural resources is a "highly visibility" job, many tasks, such as research, are performed behind the scenes. One such task is the monitoring of radon gas and cave air quality.

CHIP CLARK

DEPRESSION-ERA MAMMOTH CAVE

The years following Collins' death were tumultuous in the Mammoth Cave area. While the Mammoth Cave National Park Association played a vital role in fund raising and donation solicitation, it was the duty of the Kentucky National Park Commission, formed in 1928, to acquire lands. Land acquisition was a touchy subject to some. Most families sold their homes willingly, but a few were forced to leave through the use of eminent domain.

In 1933, the Civilian Conservation Corps (CCC) began a nine-year stint at Mammoth Cave. Corpsmen assisted in forest restoration and developed both surface and cave facilities. Rebuilding cave trails, constructing buildings, and creating roads, these men performed numerous duties that contributed toward the creation of Mammoth Cave National Park. The four camps of "CCC boys" at Mammoth Cave represented one of the most extensive CCC projects in Kentucky. Park visitors and National Park Service personnel are still benefiting from their nine years of dedication. Some of the corpsmen, like James "Tubby" Skaggs, went on to become lifetime National Park Service employees.

SUGGESTED READING

BRUCKER, ROGER W. and RICHARD A. WATSON. *The Longest Cave*. New York: Alfred A. Knopf, 1976.

BRYANT, GWYNNE, ed. *The Croghans of Locust Grove: Last Home of General George Rogers Clark*. Cincinnati, Ohio: Creative Company, 1988.

BULLITT, ALEXANDER CLARK. *Rambles in Mammoth Cave*. St. Louis: Cave Books, 1985.

DE PAIPE, DUANE. *Gunpowder from Mammoth Cave: The saga of Saltpetre Mining Before and During the War of 1812*. Hays, Kansas: Cave Pearl Press, 1985.

LAWRENCE, JOE, JR., and ROGER W. BRUCKER. *The Caves Beyond*. Teaneck, New Jersey: Zephyrus Press, 1975.

MELOY, HAROLD. *Mummies of Mammoth Cave*. Shelbyville, Indiana: Micron, 1971.

MURRAY, ROBERT A. and ROGER A. BRUCKER. *Trapped!* Lexington, Ky.: University Press of Kentucky, 1979.

WATSON, PATTY JO. *Archaeology of the Mammoth Cave Area*. New York: Academic Press, 1974.

*P*ark rangers enjoy sharing the "above ground" experience with visitors who take the opportunity to camp, canoe, or hike park trails. At an evening campfire program set on a woodland stage, a park ranger interprets nineteenth-century life along the Green River.

ROBERT J. CETERA

"The years following Collins' death were tumultuous..."

*T*he cave's skintight blanket of darkness has challenged explorers for centuries. In this room "The Church," light cast by the replica of an open flame lantern illuminates a group of visitors. The beams of light are reminiscent of sunrise. The park ranger's words are enlightening, as well.

CHIP CLARK

All About Mammoth Cave

Eastern National Association

Eastern National is a not-for-profit partner of the National Park Service. By providing quality educational products and services, they assist the Service in helping visitors to better understand the park and its resources.

Through the sale of educational products and publications, Eastern National donates the profit from these sales to the National Park Service. The Service uses these funds to support their interpretive and educational programs.

At Mammoth Cave, the park has used donated funds to support a variety of programs and events. The sale of merchandise from the visitor center store and from the web site: www.eparks.com supports these programs.

Thank you for supporting Mammoth Cave National Park.

For information about the park:

Write to:
Mammoth Cave
P.O. Box 7
Mammoth Cave, KY
42259-0007
Park information #
270-758-2328
Fax #
270-758-2349
email contact
MACA_Park_Information
@nps.gov
Website:
www.nps.gov/maca

Gray squirrel
PHOTO BY
THOMAS A. SCHNEIDER

Mammoth Cave Junior Ranger

Are you ages 6 – 12 years old and want to become a Junior Ranger for Mammoth Cave National Park?

It takes a special person to understand the importance of taking care of the plants and animals that are inside as well as outside of the park, learning the history of Mammoth Cave and its surrounding area. All you have to do is purchase the Junior Ranger packet (for a nominal fee,) from the Visitor Center and complete the activities within the booklet, and take a guided tour with one of the park rangers. Explore the park above and below ground, see the many marvels that it has for you to learn and appreciate. You are that special person, become a Mammoth Cave Junior Ranger!

For those ready for more of an adventurous adventure participate in the Trog Tours and be prepared for hiking, climbing, and crawling – don't forget to wear warm clothing and sturdy shoes – safety helmets and lights are provided! (There is a fee for these tours.)

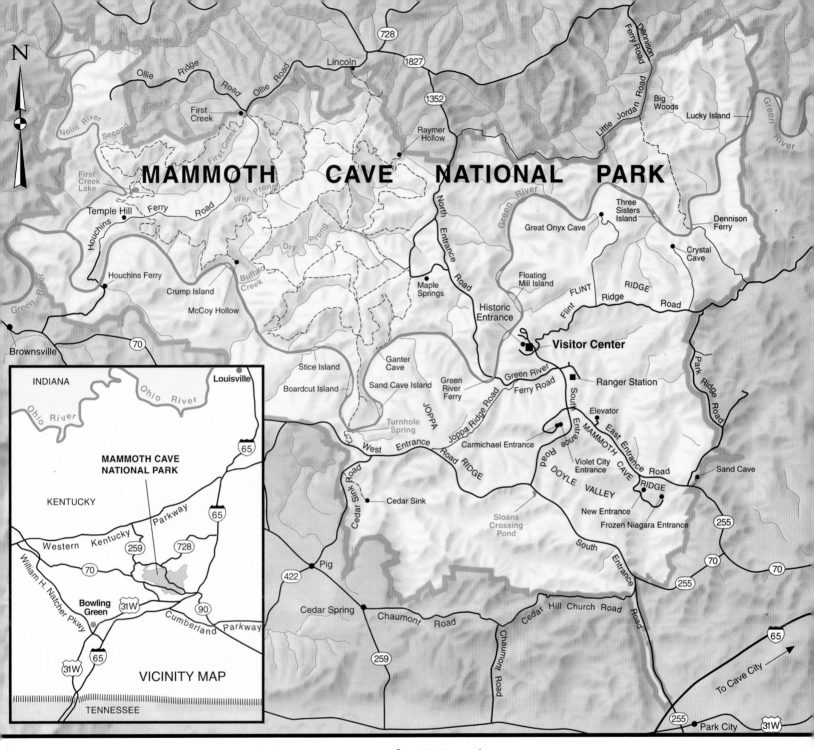

Tomorrow's Heritage

Designated a World Heritage Site by the United Nations Educational, Scientific and Cultural Organization (UNESCO) in 1981, and a Biosphere Reserve in 1990, nearly 2 million people visit the park annually. Many visit the cave, participating in one or more of the guided tours offered. Visitors respect the surface as well. They canoe the rivers, hike or camp in the backcountry, enjoy horseback rides, or relax along the river's edge. Park officials, dedicated to making facilities more accessible, have designed and installed accessible boardwalk structures for the Heritage Trail, at the Sand Cave overlook and at Sloan's Crossing Pond.

Visitors to Mammoth Cave experience the "usual" national park scene. Motorists block traffic to hurriedly snap photos of a doe and her fawn. Campers find raccoon's great fun until they try to carry off an ice chest full of food. Vistas are breath taking, summer nights are filled with the cicada's song, and the morning air is rich with the smells of coffee brewing and bacon frying in the camp-grounds.

Beneath the park's 53,000 acres lies the cave. Not just any cave, but the Mammoth Cave. This is the one that challenges professional cavers to go that extra step, squeeze through one more crawl, and climb that night-filled dome. This one is the longest cave of all. Mapped at nearly 400 miles in length, Mammoth Cave is, by far, the longest cave system in the world.

And so the saga continues. Underground rivers continue their ancient journey through rock. Calcium-laden droplets hang patiently in darkness, content in their painstaking artistry. People, still challenged by the cave, strive to meet those challenges. Today, Mammoth Cave National Park rangers search for solutions to polluted waterways. They monitor air quality and strive to protect the park's cultural resources.

But, for all the studies, research, and exploration accomplished, our greatest challenge is education. Watch more closely. See how it's done. Park rangers don't talk down to children. They drop to one knee and point out cave crickets on a wall. They show the water's path as it flows underground, carrying food to silent cave animals. They point to a blue heron in flight or to a wild turkey near the for-est's edge. At three-foot heights, the park rangers search these young eyes and smile when tiny glints of recognition give way to understanding. Through early education, children accept our challenges and, enthusiastically, they rise to meet them.

The two worlds of Mammoth Cave—one dark, one light—are eternally bound. A delicate balance must be kept to protect that unique natural resource we call Mammoth Cave. Rare life forms found 360 feet beneath the surface are protected by an exchange of ideas that occurs only 3 feet above the cool green of ferns and the yellow glow of jonquils. May we humble ourselves to meet the challenge. May conservation's torch be passed.

CHIP CLARK

The cycles of life continue as a new day dawns above the dark passages of Mammoth Cave.

KC Publications has been the leading publisher of colorful, interpretive books about National Park areas, public lands, Indian lands, and related subjects for over 40 years. We have 6 active series—over 125 titles—with Translation Packages in up to 8 languages for over half the areas we cover. Write, call, or visit our web site for our full-color catalog.

Our series are:

The Story Behind the Scenery® – Compelling stories of over 65 National Park areas and similar Public Land areas. Some with Translation Packages.

in pictures... The Continuing Story® – A companion, pictorially oriented, series on America's National Parks. All titles have Translation Packages.

For Young Adventurers™ – Dedicated to young seekers and keepers of all things wild and sacred. Explore America's Heritage from A to Z.

Voyage of Discovery® – Exploration of the expansion of the western United States.

Indian Culture and the Southwest – All about Native Americans, past and present.

Calendars – For National Parks and Southwest Indian culture, in dramatic full color, and a companion Color Your Own series, with crayons.

To receive our full-color catalog featuring over 125 titles—Books, Calendars, Screen Scenes, Videos, Audio Tapes, and other related specialty products:

Call (800-626-9673), fax (702-433-3420), write to the address below, Or visit our web site at www.kcpublications.com

Published by KC Publications, 3245 E. Patrick Ln., Suite A, Las Vegas, NV 89120.

Inside back cover:
Nature's artistic hand sculpts the delicate folds of the Drapery room's dizzying ceiling.
Photo by Ed Cooper.

Back cover:
Aging trees prayerfully pay homage to fire and water.
Photo by Robert J. Cetera.

Created, Designed, and Published in the U.S.A.
Printed by Tien Wah Press (Pte.) Ltd, Singapore
Pre-Press by United Graphic Pte. Ltd